This book belongs to:

Printed in Great Britain
by Amazon

82238434R00072